DINOSAUR PARENTS, DINOSAUR YOUNG

DINOSAUR PARENTS, DINOSAUR YOUNG

UNCOVERING THE MYSTERY OF DINOSAUR FAMILIES

BY KATHLEEN WEIDNER ZOEHFELD

WITH FULL-COLOR PAINTINGS BY PAUL CARRICK
AND LINE DRAWINGS BY BRUCE SHILLINGLAW

CLARION BOOKS • NEW YORK

In memory of C. Tyler Hill

I would like to especially thank Dr. Kenneth Carpenter of the Denver Museum of Natural History for his expert advice. Thanks also to Dr. Robert Bakker, Bruce Shillinglaw, Dr. Roland Shook, Laurie Trexler, and Dr. David Varricchio for their assistance on many research questions, as well as to Bruce Selyem of the Museum of the Rockies and to Matthew Pavlick of the American Museum of Natural History for their help with photo research. I am also indebted to the work of Roy Chapman Andrews, Dr. John Horner, and Dr. Michael Novacek. My very special thanks goes out to the late Dorothy Briley for seeing the potential in the idea. And further thanks to my wonderful editor, Jennifer Greene, and to designer Jessica Battaini and art director Joann Hill for seeing it through. Also thanks to Drew Lamm for her support in the early stages of the writing, and to my husband, Robert Zoehfeld, for being there with ideas and encouragement, beginning to end.
—K.W.Z.

Clarion Books
a Houghton Mifflin Company imprint
215 Park Avenue South, New York, NY 10003
Text copyright © 2001 by Kathleen Weidner Zoehfeld
Full-color illustrations copyright © 2001 by Paul Carrick
Line drawings copyright © 2001 by Bruce Shillinglaw
First Clarion paperback edition, 2006.

The full-color illustrations were executed in acrylic paint,
and the black-and-white illustrations were executed in pen and ink.
The text was set in 14-point Meridien.
Maps by Kayley LeFaiver.

www.clarionbooks.com

Photographs by Shackelford: 7, 8; photograph by AMNH: 10; photograph by D. Finnin: 11 bottom; photograph by Mick Ellison: 11 top;
all courtesy American Museum of Natural History, Department of Library Services
Museum of the Rockies: 23, 24
Mary Evans Picture Library: 17
Copyright © Peabody Museum of Natural History, Yale University, New Haven, Connecticut: 18
Photograph by Don Enger: 25 top; photograph by Henry Ausloos: 25 bottom; both copyright © Animals Animals
Copyright © Louie Psihoyos: 38, 40
Photographs by H. Brooks Walter, courtesy National Geographic Society: 42, 44

Printed in Singapore.

Library of Congress Cataloging-in-Publication Data

Zoehfeld, Kathleen Weidner.
Dinosaurs parents, dinosaur young : uncovering the mystery of dinosaur families / by Kathleen Weidner Zoehfeld ;
with full-color illustrations by Paul Carrick and black-and-white line drawings by Bruce Shillinglaw.
Includes bibliographical references and index.
p.   cm.
ISBN 0-395-91338-1
1. Dinosaurs—Behavior—Juvenile literature. 2. Parental behavior in animals—Juvenile literature. [1. Dinosaurs. 2. Fossils. 3. Paleontology.]
I. Carrick, Paul, ill. II. Shillinglaw, Bruce, ill. III. Title.
QE861.6.B44 Z64   2001
567.9—dc21   0-043101
CIP

CL ISBN-13: 978-0-395-91338-3   CL ISBN-10: 0-395-91338-1
PA ISBN-13: 978-0-618-75244-7   PA ISBN-10: 0-618-75244-7

TWP 10 9 8 7 6 5 4

CONTENTS

"Scientific knowledge is always tentative, always being refined. The history of science shows a progression of theories embraced for a time, only to be overturned or adjusted when contradicted by observation."

—George Smoot and Keay Davidson, *Wrinkles in Time*

1

A Big Mistake

An Oviraptor's Tale

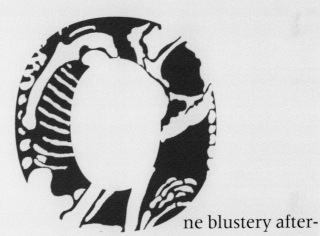

ne blustery afternoon seventy-three million years ago, a mother and father *Oviraptor* (OH-vih-RAP-tor) dug a shallow nest in the desert sand. The mother laid sixteen oval eggs in two circles—first a small circle, then a larger one around that. Then the parents scratched a thin layer of sand over their eggs to hide them.

That evening, the mother *Oviraptor* went off in search of food while the father sat down atop the nest to guard it and to keep the eggs warm. He kept a wary eye on a herd of *Protoceratops* (pro-toe-SAIR-ah-tops) milling around the shallow lake nearby. The *Protoceratops* were not interested in *him*, but if the herd began to wander in his direction, his eggs would be in danger of being trampled.

As he watched, a pack of *Velociraptor*s (vel-AH-sih-RAP-tors) leaped from the bushes and attacked a baby *Protoceratops*. The adult *Protoceratops* charged the *Velociraptor*s and drove them away from the baby. Then the *Protoceratops* encircled all their young and began to run. Within moments, one of the swift predators brought down an older *Protoceratops* who lagged behind. Together, the *Velociraptor*s dragged the carcass to a shady spot, where they could feast on it in comfort. The rest of the terrified *Protoceratops* kept running.

The father *Oviraptor* stood up to get a better view. The stampeding herd was heading directly toward his nest! The *Oviraptor* was six feet tall, and he weighed about seventy-five pounds—no match for a herd of frightened, four-hundred-pound *Protoceratops*. Still, he could not run away and let them crush his eggs. He squawked and raced toward the leader of the herd. With his three-inch-long foreclaws, he scratched the *Protoceratops*'s rough hide.

Feathers on *Oviraptor*'s body and arms may have helped it keep its eggs at the right temperature for the developing embryos.

2

The *Protoceratops* shook him off, and the *Oviraptor* hit the ground hard. Stunned and injured, the *Oviraptor* scrambed back to his nest and stood his ground. The herd veered off and thundered past him. The eggs were safe from *Protoceratops* feet. But now another danger appeared on the horizon, where fierce winds were churning up a dense cloud of sand.

As the sandstorm approached, the exhausted *Oviraptor* stretched one hand out protectively over his eggs and collapsed on his nest. Around him the sands blew and shifted. Soon the terrifying storm was upon him. Within a few hours, the father *Oviraptor* and his eggs were completely buried.

Run as they might, the *Protoceratops* and the *Velociraptor*s could not escape the raging sandstorm either. As the thick cloud of sand overtook them, they found it harder and harder to breathe. The sand rose above their ankles, their knees, their necks. They tried to swim up through the shifting sand, but it was too late. Soon they, too, were buried.

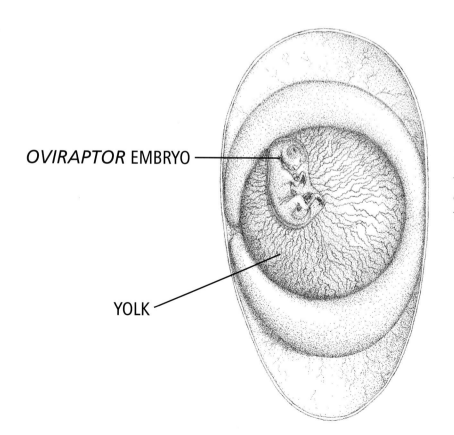

OVIRAPTOR EMBRYO

YOLK

Like bird eggs, dinosaur eggs had hard shells. The yolk of the egg provided the embryo, or growing baby, with all the food and moisture it needed.

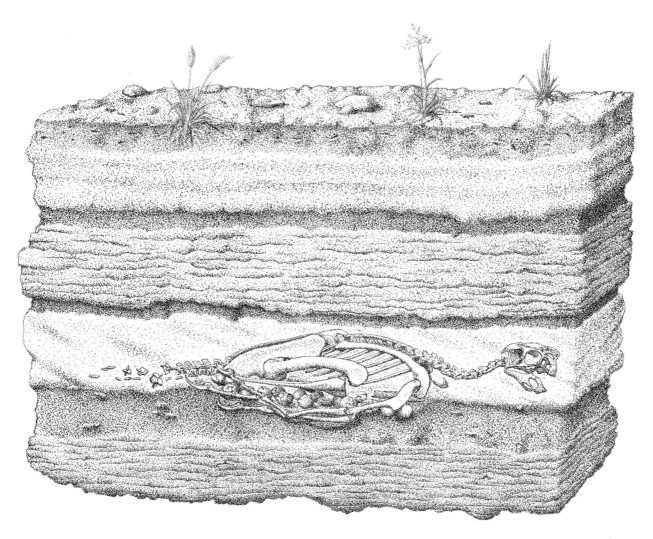

Over the course of months and years, the bones and eggs of the buried dinosaurs were fossilized. For a fossil to form, layer after layer of sand and soil must accumulate over the bones and press down upon them. The pressure causes the particles of sand to squeeze closer and closer together until the bones are encased in solid rock. If the local groundwater contains dissolved minerals, the minerals will fill up the tiny pores in the bones where the softer materials have rotted away, making the fossils as heavy as rock.

The next morning, the mother *Oviraptor* returned to the area. The features of the landscape were covered by a deep layer of sand. The air was still, and the world seemed strangely quiet. All day she searched for her nest and her mate, but she could find no trace of either. So, reluctantly, she moved on—on to search for a new mate and to build a new nest.

THE GOBI DESERT: 1923

Seventy-three million years after this deadly sandstorm, a group of paleontologists sent by the American Museum of Natural History in New York was exploring the Gobi Desert in Mongolia, not far from the spot where the *Oviraptor*s had nested.

On July 13, 1923, the group was digging in the area of Bayn Dzak, the spectacular formation also called the Flaming Cliffs. Assistant paleontologist George Olsen discovered three cracked fossil eggs beside a small sandstone ledge. When he brushed away the loose sand on top of the ledge, Olsen found the broken skeleton of a strange, unknown dinosaur. One of its long, three-fingered hands was stretched out across the ledge. Hidden inside the ledge, beneath the creature's hand, were thirteen more eggs. The oval eggs seemed to have been placed in two concentric circles—one circle inside the other.

The expedition leader, Roy Chapman Andrews, and his chief paleontologist, Walter Granger, were excited by the unusual find. Before long, the scientists discovered that the crinkly textured, seven-inch-long oval eggs were fairly common in the area. Later that summer, and during the summer of 1925, several more nests were uncovered. Since the fossilized remains of many *Protoceratops*, both young and old, were found near the nests, the scientists reasoned that the eggs must be *Protoceratops* eggs.

Back in New York, Andrews and the other scientists showed their new dinosaur to the president of the museum, Henry Fairfield Osborn. Dr. Osborn studied the creature's bones. He noted its long sturdy hind legs, its relatively short arms, with hands capable of grasping, and thick long tail. The skull had a high crest, big eye sockets, and a weird, toothless beak. Later study revealed two bony prongs growing down from the roof of its mouth. No one had ever seen a skull like this one before.

Roy Chapman Andrews's caravan winds toward the Flaming Cliffs of the Gobi. (*Gobi* in the Mongolian language means "waterless place.")

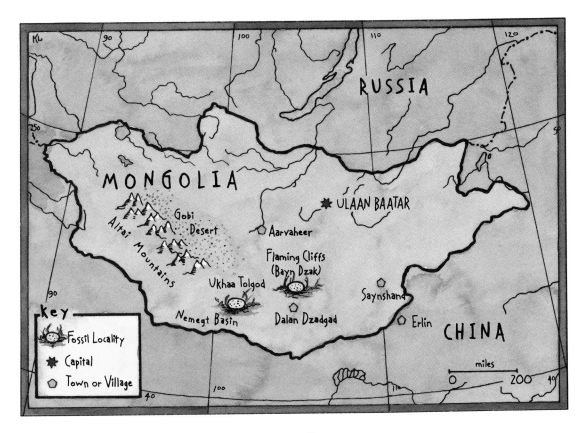

Mongolia

These were the first dinosaur eggs ever identified. Large fossil egg fragments were discovered in France in 1859, but at the time no one realized they were from dinosaur eggs. People had long guessed that dinosaurs laid eggs, but the Gobi eggs were the first real proof.

Drs. Osborn and Granger observed that the dinosaur with the bizarre beak and grasping hands seemed well-designed for egg eating. Since it had been found lying atop a clutch of what they believed were *Protoceratops* eggs, they imagined that it had been caught in the act of robbing the nest—overwhelmed by a sudden sandstorm. Dr. Osborn named the creature *Oviraptor*, from the Latin words meaning "egg thief." For seventy years, people told the story of the egg stealer, sneaking around the *Protoceratops* nests by night, cracking the tough eggshells with its horny beak and lapping up the contents.

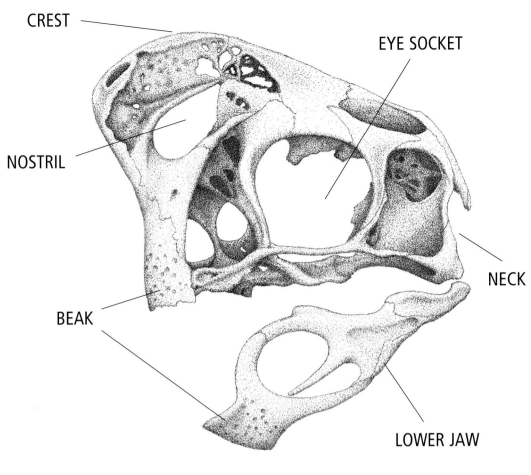

CREST

EYE SOCKET

NOSTRIL

NECK

BEAK

LOWER JAW

Oviraptor's skull

THE GOBI DESERT: 1993

In 1993, that story changed forever. Mark Norell, Michael Novacek, and other paleontologists from the American Museum of Natural History and the Mongolian Academy of Sciences were exploring the Gobi that summer. In a place called Ukhaa Tolgod, about two hundred miles west of the Flaming Cliffs, they discovered a sandy flat, rich with fossils of all kinds. Like the scientists of the Andrews expedition, they found several circular nests of the seven-inch-long oval *"Protoceratops"* eggs.

In one of these nests, Dr. Norell found a rare treasure: a broken egg filled with the tiny bones of a dinosaur embryo. Right away the scientists could see that these eggs did not belong to the herbivorous *Protoceratops,* as had long been assumed. The tiny three-toed feet told them that the eggs belonged to a carnivore of some kind.

Just a few days after this breathtaking discovery, crew members Luis Chiappe and Amy Davidson began excavating a large, fifteen-foot-long *Oviraptor* skeleton that Dr. Norell had discovered earlier. They were astonished to discover that it, too, seemed to be lying atop a nest of the familiar seven-inch-long oval eggs.

Their *Oviraptor* naturally reminded them of the egg thief that Andrews's crew had found. Was this just a strange coincidence? The odds of finding two *Oviraptor*s caught in the act of raiding a nest were astronomical. But if

Dr. Norell hunting fossils
in Ukhaa Tolgod

The fossil egg containing the famous *Oviraptor* embryo. Above right is a tiny jaw of a juvenile carnivore (thought to be a troodontid) found in the *Oviraptor* nest.

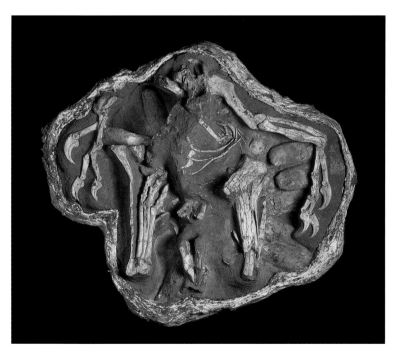

The nesting *Oviraptor,* sometimes called "Big Mama," found at Ukhaa Tolgod in 1993

11

the eggs were not *Protoceratops* eggs, which dinosaur did they belong to? The solution to this mystery was not to come for many months.

The precious specimens were wrapped up and shipped back to the Museum of Natural History in New York for study. That fall, Davidson, an expert preparator, began to pick away some of the soft sandstone around the embryo's delicate bones. After months of painstaking work, the bones and distinctive skull were revealed: What Dr. Norell had discovered was the world's first *Oviraptor* embryo. Scientists had finally identified the famous Gobi eggs with certainty.

The stories people had told about *Oviraptor,* the egg thief, were incorrect. Now we tell the tale of the *Oviraptor* parent who guarded its nest at all costs. *Oviraptor* will keep its name forever—even though, to be fair, it should probably be changed to the Latin words for "nest protector."

2

Questions and More Questions

cientists are always searching for clues that will help them answer their questions in better, more accurate ways. Often, though, once one question is answered, new and even more difficult questions leap to mind.

Before Andrews, Granger, and Olsen discovered nests full of dinosaur eggs, every paleontologist's question was: "Did dinosaurs lay eggs?" The discoveries of the first Gobi expedition proved once and for all that the answer to that question is yes. Then the question became: "Which dinosaurs laid which eggs?" Andrews and his colleagues could not be absolutely sure that the eggs they discovered were really *Protoceratops* eggs.

They based their theory on the evidence they had found up to that point. But, as scientists, they knew that until the bones of an embryo were identified inside one of the eggs, no one could be certain.

Today we have clear evidence that tells us the most abundant eggs in the Gobi were, without a doubt, laid by *Oviraptor*. Now the questions are even trickier: What were *Oviraptor* families like? How did they behave? Can evidence be found that will tell us about the lives of these ancient creatures?

If we could travel back in time and live among the dinosaurs, or if someday scientists discovered a way to clone dinosaurs from substances in their bones, then we could observe firsthand how dinosaurs reared their young. We could become familiar with their colors and textures and smells. We could listen to the sounds they made. But so far, no time machine has been invented, and the possibility of cloning dinosaurs in the near future seems remote.

Today's paleontologists must do exactly what Andrews and his colleagues did. They must collect every fossil clue they can find and, from those clues, develop a theory, or hypothesis. A hypothesis is a story scientists create to answer a particular question or set of questions. A good hypothesis is based on clues that scientists have gathered and studied carefully. But even good hypotheses must be questioned. Often the discovery of a new clue challenges an accepted theory. If the new clue does not fit, scientists must revise their hypothesis.

MORE *OVIRAPTOR* CLUES

The discovery of the true occupants of the seven-inch-long oval eggs of the Gobi has forced us to change the story about the egg thief. But is *Oviraptor*'s new story *exactly* the right story? It is certainly much closer to the

Oviraptor parents feeding a baby carnivore to their own young

truth. But before we have the whole picture, even more questions will need to be answered.

Like some modern birds, did father and mother *Oviraptor*s work together to guard the nest, bring home food, and raise their young? Or was the mother or father left to do the job alone? Did *Oviraptor* parents gather in colonies to lay their eggs, or did they prefer solitary nesting sites?

If *Oviraptor*s did not eat "*Protoceratops* eggs," then what *did* they eat? In the nest that contained the embryo, scientists found two tiny skulls of baby meat-eating dinosaurs. Did *Oviraptor* parents raid *Troodon* or *Velociraptor* nests and return with tiny hatchlings to feed their babies? That is one possibility. Or perhaps the young carnivores died trying to raid the *Oviraptor* nest.

Over the years, as more clues are found, our *Oviraptor*'s tale may change again.

Perhaps the most amazing thing about the *Oviraptor* clues is that they tell us something about the dinosaur's behavior. Fossils of adult skeletons can tell us about the size and shape of creatures, but they cannot tell us how those creatures were born, how they grew up, how they related to each other, or how they took care of their young. Only more nesting sites, more babies, and more embryos can help answer these questions.

The discovery of a second *Oviraptor* that seemed to be protecting its nest was extremely exciting. However, some cautious scientists considered that the creatures' nearness to their nests could have been simply a coincidence. Perhaps the moment the mothers finished laying their eggs, sandstorms (which were common at the time) or sandy mudslides overwhelmed them. The first *Oviraptor*'s bones appear to have been broken. So another possibility was that an injury prevented that parent from attempting to flee.

Since Dr. Norell's discovery in 1993, though, several more nesting *Oviraptor* fossils have been found in the Gobi, as well as one in northern China. In all cases, the creatures are hunkered down on their nests with arms folded back over their eggs, exactly the way chickens and many other brooding birds fold their wings. Either violent sandstorms or mudslides were responsible for their deaths. Clearly, *Oviraptor*s did sit on their nests to hatch their eggs. They must have stuck by them with great tenacity—even in the face of bad weather and terrible dangers. Brooding behavior in *Oviraptor* was not the exception; it was the rule.

LIZARD OR BIRD?

Today, scientists are sure that at least some dinosaurs were protective parents. But for a long time, scientists did not even imagine that this could be true. In 1842, on the basis of fossil teeth and a few fossil bones from the three known

Fig. 195. L'Iguanodon et le Mégalosaure. (Période crétacée inférieure.)

As evidenced in this 1866 drawing, paleontologists of the nineteenth century pictured the dinosaurs *Iguanodon* and *Megalosaurus* as quadrupeds, or four-legged creatures. Based on more recent fossil evidence, we know that these creatures were bipedal, or two-legged.

species of that time—*Megalosaurus* (MEG-gah-loh-soar-us), *Iguanodon* (ih-GWAH-no-don), and *Hylaeosaurus* (HI-lee-oh-soar-us)—paleontologists noted that these huge, mysterious creatures had many lizardlike features. Sir Richard Owen, a prominent British paleontologist, coined the term *dinosaur* from Greek words meaning "fearfully great lizard."

From that time right up until the 1960s, most scientists thought of dinosaurs as enormous overgrown lizards. A few artists even showed these ponderous creatures with the sprawling or splayed stance of lizards—a position that would have been impossible, considering their tremendous weight.

Since all the clues seemed to indicate that dinosaurs *looked* like lizards, scientists theorized that they *behaved* like lizards, too. Lizards are part of the reptile class, which includes turtles, snakes, and crocodilians. Although some crocodilian mothers are known to guard their nests and even to watch over their young for the first year of life, nearly all other reptiles alive today lay eggs and immediately abandon them. Lizard, snake, and turtle hatchlings have to fend for themselves in a harsh world. For scientists in the 1800s and early 1900s, it was impossible to imagine reptiles—which are generally sluggish, cold-blooded, and even a bit dim-witted—bonding in pairs or in larger social groups for the purpose of building nests, bringing home food to their babies, and protecting them from enemies.

A few scientists at that time pointed out that dinosaurs shared some physical similarities with birds. Some even suggested that modern-day birds may have evolved from dinosaurs. But the evidence seemed slim, and these observations went largely ignored until the 1960s, when Yale University paleontologist John Ostrom discovered a fearsome dinosaur in the badlands

Mounted skeletons of *Deinonychus*

1 S-SHAPED NECK
2 PRESENCE OF FIVE HIP VERTEBRAE
3 WALKING ON THREE TOES
4 SIMPLE HINGED ANKLES
5 BACKWARD-POINTING PELVIS BONES
6 ARMS CAPABLE OF FOLDING
7 LONG, SKINNY SHOULDER BLADES

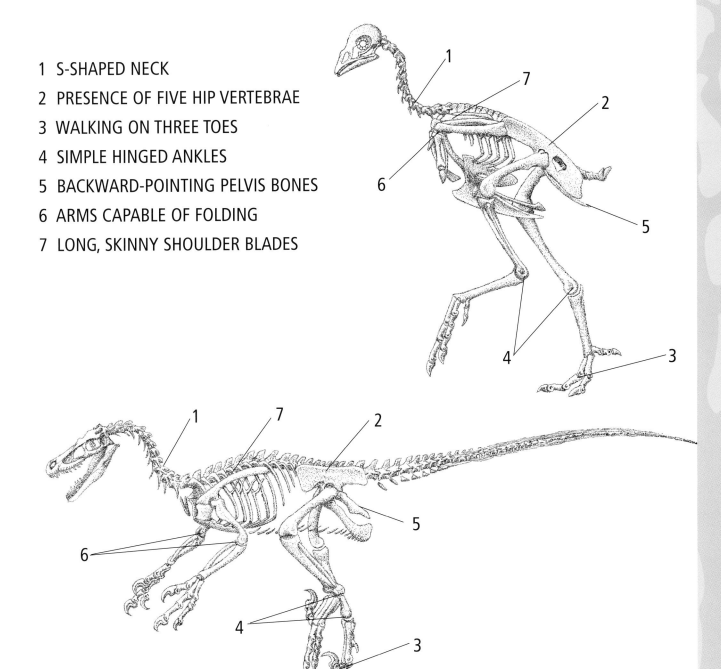

This comparison of a bird skeleton (above) to the skeleton of a theropod dinosaur (below) shows the shared characteristics that give both good bipedal locomotion. Bipedal locomotion would have freed the forelimbs of birds to evolve into wings.

of Montana. He named his find *Deinonychus* (dy-NON-ik-us), or "terrible claw."

Deinonychus was a relatively small dinosaur, about the size of a grown man. It had sharp teeth, long powerful legs, and huge sickle-shaped claws on its hands and birdlike feet. This lean, agile carnivore, a member of the dinosaur group called theropods, helped convince Ostrom that dinosaurs were not sluggish, cold-blooded animals like reptiles, but, rather, active, warm-blooded creatures like mammals or birds.

Ostrom also observed that *Deinonychus* was similar in many ways to *Archaeopteryx* (ar-kee-OP-teh-rix), a 150-million-year-old feathered creature found in the late 1800s in layered limestone rocks near Solnhofen, Germany, that had both birdlike and reptilian characteristics. Ostrom and his student, Robert Bakker, hypothesized that a dinosaur similar to *Deinonychus*, perhaps an early *Deinonychus* cousin, may have been the first bird ancestor.

What if dinosaurs were warm-blooded, swift, intelligent creatures—the precursors of today's birds? By the 1970s, many paleontologists were captivated by this new way of thinking about dinosaurs. A few began to theorize that at least some dinosaurs behaved the way birds do: forming social groups, making and tending nests, and taking care of their babies. At that time, the major *Oviraptor* discoveries were still more than twenty years in the future. The fossil evidence that might help explain dinosaur behavior was scarce, to say the least. For many years, all scientists could do was search and wonder.

3
The Good Mother Lizard

he 1990s discoveries of *Oviraptor*s caught in the act of brooding their eggs gave scientists a wealth of information. But the first important discovery to shed light on dinosaur behavior had occurred in 1978 in the badlands of northwestern Montana.

During a summer vacation, John Horner, then a fossil preparator at Princeton University, and his college friend, science teacher Robert Makela, stopped by a rock shop in the little town of Bynum to help the owners, John and Marion Brandvold, identify a fossil. Happy for their help, the Brandvolds brought out a few more fossils that had puzzled them. Among them Horner saw a bit of thighbone, a piece of rib, and a partial jaw from what was certainly a duckbill dinosaur. Common enough—except that these were miniature in size! They could only be from baby duckbills, something Horner had long hoped to find. When he and Makela excitedly told the Brandvolds how important these fossils were, the couple led the paleontologists to the site where they had found the little bones.

There, Horner and Makela discovered what looked like a dinosaur nest—a circular, six-foot-wide, three-foot-deep depression in the ground, filled with bits of fossilized eggshell and the bones of baby dinosaurs. Nearby they found the skull of an adult dinosaur that must have been a parent or older relative. It was a type of duckbill hadrosaur that had never been seen before.

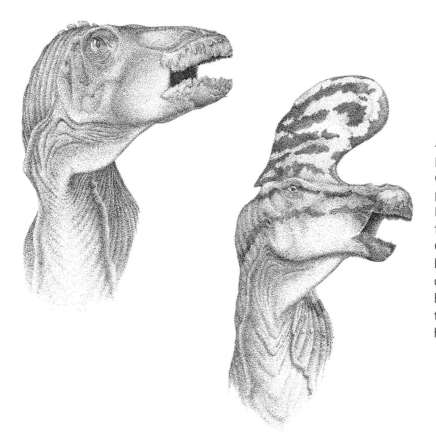

A duckbill dinosaur was a large, plant-eating dinosaur with a duck-like beak, which it used for plucking leaves and branches. Many different types of duckbills flourished toward the end of the Cretaceous Period (144 to 65 million years ago). There were two distinct types of duckbills: the hadrosaurs, with flat heads, and the lambeosaurs, with crested heads.

By 1983, Dr. Horner and his colleagues had found thirteen more nests and many more eggs and babies. The nesting site provided many clues about the family life of dinosaurs:

• The nests seemed to be evenly spaced—twenty-three feet apart.
• Bits of chewed-up fossil plants were found in one of the nests.
• In most of the nests, the eggshells were crushed rather than broken in large pieces.
• Of the nests with babies in them, the smallest babies were about fourteen inches long. The largest nestlings were about twenty-six inches long.
• The ends of the babies' leg bones were made of relatively soft, calcified cartilage rather than solid bone.

John Horner studied these clues and began to describe dinosaur families in more detail than ever before. He pictured the dry upland plain as it might have looked eighty million years ago, with a nesting ground of forty or more nests. The nests were placed just far enough apart so that the big dinosaurs did not whack each other with their tails when they turned

Dr. Horner (with colleague Karen Chin) prospecting for fossils in the dry Montana landscape near the nesting ground

The reconstructed skull of the adult hadrosaur (*Maiasaura*) found in the nesting site

around. Many modern-day birds, such as flamingos and most terns, nest in colonies like this, and the distance between their nests is always about the length of an adult bird.

The mother dinosaurs probably plucked branches with their duckbill nippers and brought them back to cover their nests. As the leaves and stems rotted, they would have given warmth to the eggs and the embryos inside them. The parents would not have been able to sit on the nests as most birds do, since the adults probably outweighed their young by several tons.

In a few of the nests, the eggs had already hatched. Because of their undeveloped bones, made up mostly of relatively soft calcified cartilage, the hatchlings wobbled like the babies of most bird species. When they tried to walk, they tipped over and fell on their snouts. They stretched their heads up toward their mothers' huge faces and squeaked hungrily.

The mothers—and maybe the fathers, too—knew what to do. They trotted to the nearby stream and nipped branches from the berry bushes. They chewed them up and carried them back to the nests in their cheeks. Or, they may have swallowed the food and then regurgitated it for their nestlings, the way many birds do.

About eighty percent of all bird species are *altricial.* Altricial babies, such as robins, hawks, and bluebirds, are born with undeveloped bones. Their necks droop and their legs wobble. These hatchlings must stay in the shelter of their nests until they are older and stronger. Until then, their parents must bring them food.

About twenty percent of all bird species are *precocial.* Precocial babies, such as ducks, chickens, and ostriches, have well-developed bones right from birth. They do not need to stay in nests. They can follow their parents around and get food for themselves with little help.

The babies devoured the food and squeaked for more. They toddled around their nests, crushing the empty eggshells under their feet. The babies grew quickly, but it would have taken several weeks, or even months, before they were big and strong enough to follow their parents to the stream. In the meantime, they needed to eat a lot.

The adult dinosaurs may have taken turns—one foraging for food while the other stayed behind to guard the nest. If they didn't watch carefully, large lizards could creep into the nest and grab a newborn. Packs of swift-footed, sharp-toothed *Troodon* (TROH-oh-don) must have stalked the area, too. If the parents were not alert, the *Troodon* could snap up several babies in a quick raid.

When the duckbill babies had grown to about two and a half feet long, they began to follow their parents out of the nest. The adults led their babies to the stream, where they learned to pluck berries on their own.

There is no reptile alive today that shares food with its young-sters. The discovery of a dinosaur that nested in groups and brought home food for its young was astonishing. These dinosaurs were acting much more like birds than reptiles.

Horner's boss back at Princeton, Don Baird, was impressed with this unique discovery, which revealed secrets about dinosaur behavior. He came up with the idea of naming the new dinosaur *Maiasaura* (MY-ah-SOAR-uh), from the Greek words meaning "good mother lizard."

With their short snouts and big round eyes, the baby *Maiasaura* must have been cute. That may not seem like a very scientific observation, but, as Dr. Horner and other scientists have noted, the cute, babyish characteristics of offspring appear to bring out nurturing instincts in many types of animal parents, including human ones.

But what happened to a young maiasaur once it had learned to find food for itself? Did it wander off to live on its own? Or did it stay with its family? No one knew for sure.

Then, between 1981 and 1984, Dr. Horner's group uncovered two large bone beds containing numerous limb bones of *Maiasaura* of different ages—from half-grown youngsters to adults. The bone beds lie less than one quarter of a mile apart, and Dr. Horner believes they may have been a part of one incredibly huge bone bed, representing a large group of maiasaurs that died all at once.

From this fossil evidence, Dr. Horner theorizes that *Maiasaura* may have gathered in herds of ten thousand or more. When the babies grew large and strong enough, their parents would have led them to their herd. Together they roamed the upland plains, stripping the berry bushes and eating the leaves of dogwoods and the needles of evergreens.

Within the herd, the youngsters may have stayed close to their parents for several years. That would have been the best protection against the powerful twenty-seven-foot-long tyrannosaurs called *Albertosaurus* (al-BER-toh-soar-us) that cruised the plains, feeding on the weaker members of the *Maiasaura* herds.

Dr. Horner's hypothesis about dinosaur life is based on a wide array of fossil evidence. Though other paleontologists continue to study the clues, interpreting the evidence in different ways, Dr. Horner forever changed our view of dinosaurs. No longer could any scientist see dinosaurs simply as the sluggish, cold-blooded, overgrown reptiles described by most scientists in the 1800s. It is clear now that, although they may have had some reptilian characteristics, dinosaurs were not reptilian in exactly the way today's reptiles are. The evidence of *Maiasaura* nesting behavior went a long way in helping convince scientists that dinosaurs were the ancestors of modern-day birds. But, as with any scientific theory, more concrete proof was needed.

4

More Evidence Rolls In

So far, Dr. Horner's discoveries of *Maiasaura* in Montana and Dr. Norell's discoveries of *Oviraptor* in the Gobi have given us our most detailed pictures of dinosaur life.

An important aspect of Dr. Horner's discoveries, as well as of the early egg discoveries in Mongolia, was that scientists who specialized in dinosaur eggs and babies were able to develop a clearer picture of what they were looking for and in what sorts of environments they might find it. Before Dr. Horner's breakthrough of the 1970s, fossils of dinosaur babies were practically unheard of. Since then, many new egg and juvenile discoveries have been made, both by Dr. Horner and by others.

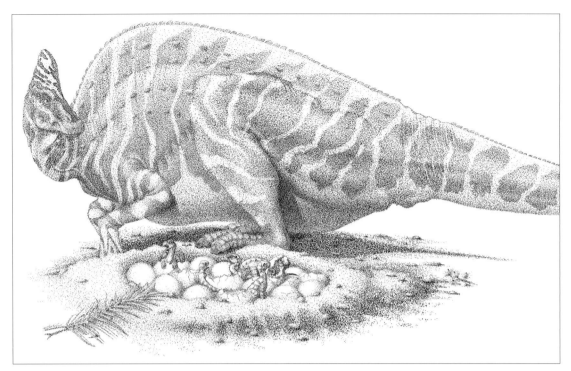

A *Hypacrosaurus* near its nest. Adult *Hypacrosaurus* could grow to be twelve feet tall and thirty feet long.

HYPACROSAURUS

In 1986, in northern Montana, Dr. Horner discovered nests, eggs, embryos, and babies of another duckbill dinosaur, a crested lambeosaur called *Hypacrosaurus* (hi-PAK-roh-soar-us). Dr. Horner and his crew found a large *Hypacrosaurus* nesting site, where a herd of a thousand or more must have returned each year to lay their eggs.

Early one nesting season, when the babies had just begun to hatch, the adults may have noticed the sky growing dark. Thick clouds of soot and ash spewed forth from volcanoes erupting just to the south of them. When hot cinders and ash began to rain down, the leaders of the herd may have used the echo chambers in their hollow nasal crests to sound a basso alarm call. They urged the mothers to abandon their nests and head north and east, away from the deadly downpour.

Today the entire nesting ground is covered by a layer of solidified volcanic sediment called bentonite, which "froze" the scene almost as it was at the time the adults abandoned it.

Not long after this discovery, Dr. Horner discovered another *Hypacrosaurus* rookery south of the first one. In Alberta, Canada, just north of the Montana border, Wendy Sloboda, then a high school student, discovered yet another.

Were the *Hypacrosaurus* helpless and nest-bound as tots, as the *Maiasaura* most certainly were? From the locations of the baby bones found around the rookeries, it is still not clear. But Dr. Horner thinks they must have been relatively helpless, like certain types of altricial birds, such as the American white pelican. These birds are nest-bound for only a short time, but for up to three months the youngsters stay together in the nesting colony, where the adults can bring them food and look after them.

Close study of the *Hypacrosaurus* babies' leg bones shows that they were made up of more calcified cartilage and less solid bone than would be expected in a precocial animal. Although there's no evidence that the little ones were completely nest-bound, they did stay within the confines of their nesting ground the way pelicans do today.

DRINKER

Robert Bakker, now the dinosaur curator for the Dinamation International Society's Wyoming chapter, believes he may have found evidence of dinosaur family life even more unusual than duckbill nesting grounds.

In 1992, at Como Bluff, Wyoming, he discovered fossils of a previously little-known hypsilophodont named *Drinker nisti*. Some of the *Drinker* bones were scattered across the landscape. Most were broken and tooth-marked by predators. However, Dr. Bakker also discovered a group of eighteen to twenty more complete *Drinker* skeletons. The members of the

Hypacrosaurus embryo

group ranged in age from quarter-grown youngsters to adults, and they were tightly crouched together, side by side, in what appears to have been an underground burrow. Since then, four more of the oval-shaped burrows have been uncovered.

Dr. Bakker theorizes that these small herbivores browsed in their warm, swampy environment, sticking together in close-knit family groups. Their long, spreading four-toed hind feet would have helped them walk efficiently in marshy terrain. And their hind claws would have been well suited for digging.

In order to avoid predators, the little *Drinker* may have dug burrows, where they could snuggle together safely in groups of anywhere from five to thirty-five individuals.

As paleontologists gather more clues, we may find that not only *Maiasaura, Hypacrosaurus,* and *Drinker* but also many other types of duck-bills and hypsilophodonts were attentive parents.

ANOTHER MISTAKE

All duckbills and hypsilophodonts are herbivores. Dr. Norell's *Oviraptor* embryo was the first embryo of a carnivorous theropod dinosaur ever found. His discoveries revealed the mistake that Andrews and Osborn made in describing *Oviraptor* as an egg thief rather than an egg protector. Dr. Norell's discoveries also led Dr. Horner to realize that he had made a startingly similar mistake about another theropod in Montana.

Near the *Maiasaura* nesting grounds is a small rounded hill called Egg Mountain. Here, in the early 1980s, Dr. Horner found a colony of a dozen egg clutches of what everyone thought was a hypsilophodont called *Orodromeus* (or-oh-DROH-mee-us). Dr. Horner and his colleagues came to this conclusion because the site was filled almost exclusively with the bones of young *Orodromeus*.

In 1993, not long after Mark Norell's embryo and nesting *Oviraptor* came to light, David Varricchio, one of Dr. Horner's graduate students at the time, found a few bones from a *Troodon* lying atop a clutch of the so-called *Orodromeus* eggs. Was this a case of *Troodon* raiding an *Orodromeus* nest? Dr. Norell's recent discovery made Dr. Horner begin to doubt his 1980s conclusion as to the identity of the eggs.

Dr. Horner knew that the only sure way to identify which dinosaur laid which eggs is to identify the embryo inside one. He asked Carrie Ancell, an expert fossil preparator at the Museum of the Rockies, to begin carefully removing the hardened sediment around one of the *"Orodromeus"* embryos. By 1996, Ancell had the answer: Dr. Varricchio's *Troodon* was not raiding an *Orodromeus* nest. The eggs were not *Orodromeus* after all—they were *Troodon*. Was the *Troodon* brooding its eggs exactly the way *Oviraptor* did? Drs. Horner and Varricchio think so. But *Troodon* fossils are extremely rare. Scientists will need to search out more evidence before we can be absolutely sure.

Were smaller dinosaurs like *Troodon* and *Oviraptor,* who sat on their nests to hatch their eggs, warm-blooded? The body heat of a warm-blooded parent is helpful for brooding eggs. Otherwise, constant heat must be provided by another source, such as rotting vegetation, as was probably the case with the *Maiasaura,* and as is the case with today's large, mound-building birds, as well as with all cold-blooded crocodilians.

Close study of the embryonic leg bones tell us that, unlike the *Maiasaura* and probably the *Hypacrosaurus, Troodon* babies were precocial—that is, they broke out of their eggs and hit the ground running. Nevertheless, Dr. Horner wondered if their parents may have tended them to some extent after birth, the way many precocial bird parents do.

Troodon, a theropod related to *Deinonychus* and *Oviraptor*, was eight feet long and had teeth like steak knives—just right for snapping up young *Orodromeus* to feed to their own babies. Of all the dinosaurs, *Troodon* had the largest brain in relation to its body size. Scientists think it must have been a smart and skillful predator.

In dinosaur times, Egg Mountain was not a mountain. Dr. Horner believes it may have been a low-lying island in a shallow lake. The island would have been the equivalent of a large playpen for the *Troodon* babies, helping to keep them safe from predators while the adults were off hunting. Dr. Horner envisions the piles of *Orodromeus* bones collecting around the *Troodon's* island as these intelligent hunters brought *Orodromeus* prey home to feed their voracious young.

As more and more nesting sites are found and as more embryo, baby, and juvenile fossils are identified properly, scientists are beginning to fill in the details in our picture of dinosaur life. Fossils of adult dinosaurs have shown us that theropod dinosaurs had some similarities to birds in their body structures. Theropod eggshells also show a similar structure to those of birds. And now the clues that tell us something about dinosaur *behavior*—the nesting sites, embryos, and babies—have added substantial support to the theory that dinosaurs were the ancient ancestors of today's birds.

5

Tiny Babies in a Land of Giants

Troodon and *Oviraptor* were relatively small dinosaurs. A full-grown *Troodon* weighed about one hundred pounds, and an *Oviraptor* weighed about seventy-five. Their two- to three-pound babies may have safely hopped around near them, like chicks around a large hen. *Maiasaura,* however, at six thousand pounds, were much heavier. Consider again how tiny the three- to four-pound hadrosaur hatchlings were compared with their parents. The little hatchlings wouldn't have been safe under the feet of the enormous adults. Staying in their nests probably helped the *Maiasaura* babies avoid being trampled. In a land of giants, growing quickly may have been another strong survival benefit.

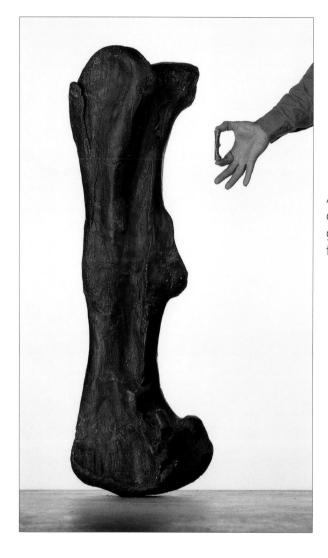

At birth, a hadrosaur's upper leg bone was small—only about three inches long. By the time it had grown to adult size, it would have been about four feet long and immensely strong and stout.

Warm-blooded creatures such as mammals and birds grow quickly from birth to maturity. Once they reach adulthood, their growth stops. Most reptiles, on the other hand, grow slowly from birth and continue to grow throughout their entire lives. The older a crocodile is, for instance, the bigger it gets. Scientists have wondered if dinosaurs grew quickly, like mammals and birds, or if they grew slowly and steadily, like reptiles.

THE LARGEST OF THEM ALL

Using powerful microscopes and computer-aided technologies, scientists are looking more closely at how dinosaur babies grew. By studying paper-thin slices of fossil bone under intense magnification, scientists can tell how much blood supply the bones were getting when the dinosaur died. Bones showing a large blood supply were in the process of growing quickly. Those with a much smaller blood supply were growing slowly or had stopped growing. For each type of dinosaur, the more specimens of different ages and sizes scientists find, the more they will be able to determine its rate of growth.

Using these methods, scientist Kristi Curry has been able to advance our understanding of the growth patterns of sauropod dinosaurs. The long-necked, pillar-legged sauropods grew to be even larger than the hadrosaurs—larger, in fact, than any land animal that has ever lived.

How big was a newly hatched sauropod baby? The baby had to fit inside an egg, so it had to have been very small compared with its parents. An eggshell must be both thick enough to keep the egg from breaking and thin enough to let oxygen in for the developing embryo. The larger the egg, the thicker the shell must be to hold the egg together. No egg can be much more than two feet in diameter. If it were larger, the shell would be too thick, and the living creature inside would smother.

Sauropod trackways, or paths, have been discovered that show the tracks of half-grown youngsters alongside the tracks of adults. And the fossil bones of a few very young sauropods have been found close to adult bones. From this evidence some scientists have hypothesized that the sauropod youngsters traveled with the adults in small herds, where they would have been protected from enemies. But could the tiny sauropod hatchlings also have moved along with the herds? Were they watched over by their parents or left to themselves? Were they fed by their parents, like fast-growing bird babies? Or did they get their own food, like the chicks of the highly precocial mound-building birds or the slower-growing reptile babies? Did they grow to adult size quickly and then stop? Or did they continue to grow throughout their lives?

In southern Montana, in the summer of 1994, Kristi Curry and her crew excavated a bone bed containing the fossils of a large group of young *Apatosaurus* (ah-PAT-oh-soar-us) that had died about 150 million years ago. As a graduate student at the State University of New York at Stony Brook, Curry spent time in the laboratory studying the bones of these sauropods in hopes of answering some of these questions.

These dinosaur eggs, called *Macroelongatoolithus xixiaensis,* were discovered in the Xixia Basin in China, and are among the largest eggs ever discovered. From observing the remains of an embryo, scientists think the eggs belonged to a type of giant *Oviraptor.*

Apatosaurus, formerly known as *Brontosaurus,* is one of the best-known members of the sauropod group.

From observing the amount of blood supply to the bones, Curry hypothesized that *Apatosaurus,* much like mammals such as cows, grew quickly until they were half-grown (about thirty feet in length). Perhaps *Apatosaurus* parents tended a group of babies in a nesting area, feeding them and protecting them until they were half-grown—big enough to move along with the herd without being trampled.

Up until 1998, the sauropod trackways and Curry's growth studies were among the few major clues available about sauropod lives. But that year, scientists from the American Museum of Natural History and from the Carmen Funes Museum in Plaza Huincul, Argentina, made a remarkable discovery.

In the dry red badlands of Patagonia, the scientists found a vast landscape, nearly one square mile, strewn with thousands of round, grapefruit-size "stones." When Luis Chiappe from the Museum of Natural History took a close look at one of these gray stippled "stones," he knew right away that

South America

Dr. Chiappe searches for more eggs in the badlands of Patagonia's Rio Colorado formation, where the sauropod nesting site was found.

they were dinosaur eggs. About seventy million years ago, during the Late Cretaceous Period—about the same time that the *Maiasaura* were nesting in North America and the *Oviraptor* in Asia—this landscape, too, was an enormous nesting ground.

Dr. Chiappe wondered what kind of dinosaur had laid the eggs. When he and his team returned home to New York, they took several of the small fossils to an expert preparator at Yale University's Peabody Museum in New Haven, Connecticut. After weeks of painstaking work, the preparator had exciting news. Some of the eggs were so well preserved that they still contained the tiny embryonic bones, including skull bones, and even bits of skin from the original occupants. There was no doubt about it: These were sauropod eggs—the first eggs ever positively identified as sauropod.

The embryonic bones alone did not provide Dr. Chiappe with enough information to indentify the exact type of sauropod. But one of the eggs contained at least thirty-two embryonic teeth, each about as small and skinny as the tip of a pin. Most sauropods have broad, flat teeth. The only sauropods from the Cretaceous Period that have pencil-like teeth like these were the titanosaurs.

Argentinosaurus (ar-jen-TEEN-oh-soar-us), among the largest of all sauropods, and the more moderately sized *Saltasaurus* (SALT-ah-SOAR-us) and *Neuquenosaurus* (NYOO-kyen-oh-SOAR-us) are sauropods that had already been discovered in Argentina and are members of the titanosaur family. Sauropods flourished in the Jurassic Period (206 to 144 million years ago), but a few, such as the titanosaurs, lived on into the Cretaceous Period. Titanosaurs were the last surviving members of the sauropod group.

When Dr. Chiappe studied the fossilized skin of his newly found embryos under an electron microscope, he discovered that the pattern of scales on the infant skin closely matched the pattern of the armored skin of an adult *Saltasaurus.* It seems most likely that Dr. Chiappe's sauropod babies

A fragment of a sauropod egg from the Patagonia site

were members of the titanosaur family—perhaps *Saltasaurus.* But more complete embryos will have to be discovered before we can be certain.

From the depth and layering of the fossil eggs in the nesting ground, Dr. Chiappe thinks that the titanosaur parents returned to this same area time after time to lay their eggs. One fateful season, though, the river bordering the nesting grounds overflowed its banks and blanketed the entire rookery with mud. Whether the adults would have normally stayed near their eggs is not known. So far, no adult bones have been found in or near the nursery. Perhaps in this case, the adults simply left the area as the floodwaters rose.

Perhaps titanosaur parents laid their eggs in a communal nesting ground, but then, like most of today's reptiles, left them to hatch and the babies to fend for themselves. The hatchlings would have been vulnerable to predators, and many would have been picked off; but there would have been thousands of them, and the next generation would have been assured by sheer numbers. Like reptiles, the babies may have grown slowly and kept to themselves.

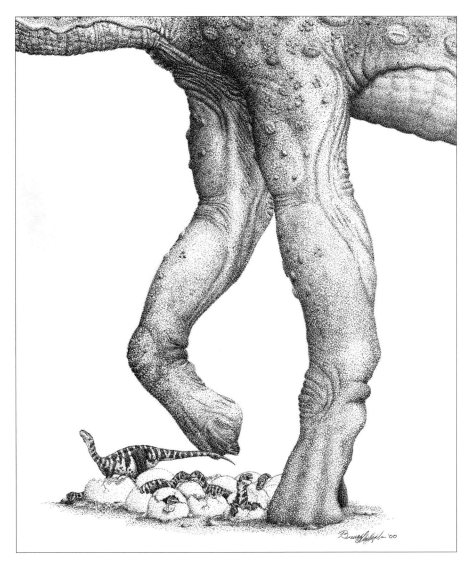

A grown-up titanosaur, which may have been more than forty-five feet long and weighed over one hundred thousand pounds, is shown here watching over its pint-size babies. The size of its eggs—a mere six inches in diameter—suggests that the hatchlings could have been no more than fifteen inches long.

Or maybe, more like birds, the adults gathered near the nesting grounds to bring food to their youngsters and to keep them from harm. Like Kristi Curry's *Apatosaurus,* the young may have grown relatively quickly and then joined the adult herd for the rest of their lives.

As yet, no one knows exactly how these supergiants related to each other, found and ate enough food, stayed safe, and grew to such huge proportions. The tantalizing fossil evidence in this Patagonia nesting ground will lure scientists back for many years to come, as will the rich fossil beds in North America and Asia.

6
The Future of Exploration

ack in 1842, when the mysterious beasts *Iguanodon, Megalosaurus,* and *Hylaeosaurus* were grouped together under the name *dinosaur,* or "fearfully great lizard," people naturally developed a mental image of dinosaurs as huge, brutish, sluggish reptiles. It was an image that was hard to shake. Today, in the light of the overwhelming new evidence, we know that view was inaccurate. In science, as in any endeavor, it is easy to make mistakes. One way scientists guard against mistakes is to practice what is called the *null hypothesis,* which means, in Dr. Horner's words, "to actively seek evidence that might contradict what we would like most to believe."

Thanks to the evidence unearthed since Dr. Horner's *Maiasaura* discoveries, we can no longer hold on to the old view of dinosaurs. With the new evidence in hand, most scientists now think of dinosaurs as the ancestors of our modern-day birds. In fact, instead of "fearfully great lizards," perhaps we should rename them "fearfully great bird-beasts"! Still, scientists find much to debate concerning the true nature of dinosaurs. Today, the dinosaur/bird theory may be the theory we "would like most to believe."

One rare fossil—a theropod called *Scipionyx* (SHIP-ee-AH-nix)—found in 1983 in limestone deposits near Naples, Italy, may, according to some scientists, cast a ray of doubt on the popular theory. This particular *Scipionyx* specimen is, coincidentally, a baby. But what makes the fossil unique is that clear impressions of the animal's internal organs have been preserved. No other known dinosaur fossil shows internal organs in such well preserved detail.

The team of scientists that studied the fossil in 1998 claim that *Scipionyx*'s colon and liver show characteristics unique to crocodilians and very different from those of birds. They argue that this fossil presents evidence that dinosaurs were *not* bird ancestors. However, most scientists see this as one small clue amid a profusion of more convincing ones.

What discoveries will the next one hundred years bring? No doubt, as scientists find more clues, theories about what kind of creatures dinosaurs were will continue to change.

Sir Richard Owen and his contemporaries would be astonished to see what we now know about the lives of *Oviraptor, Maiasaura, Hypacrosaurus, Drinker, Troodon,* and the titanosaurs. But these are only a few of the hundreds of types of dinosaurs that existed. Given another hundred years, will we get to know *all* dinosaurs as well as we know these? Will we find out that many, or even most, dinosaurs were protective parents? Or will we find that it was only a few?

It may seem unsurprising to discover that *Oviraptor*s, with their big eyes and beaky faces, were birdlike parents. But it is difficult to imagine a tiny-brained *Stegosaurus* (STEG-oh-SOAR-us), for example, even remembering where she laid her eggs. And the biggest, fiercest theropods, such as *Tyrannosaurus rex* (ty-RAN-oh-SOAR-us REX)—what kind of parents might they have been?

No stegosaur or tyrannosaur nesting sites have yet been found. But in 1990, amateur paleontologist Susan Hendrickson found a few interesting clues about *Tyrannosaurus*. Near the town of Faith, South Dakota, she uncovered the remains of a *Tyrannosaurus rex.* The skeleton was so complete and well preserved that the collectors who excavated it believed they could tell it was a female. They nicknamed her "Sue," after the paleontologist who found her. They were amazed to discover, next to Sue, bones from three other tyrannosaurs: the lower leg bones of a smaller male, part of the skull of a youngster, and part of the skull of one so small that it must have been a baby. The baby would have weighed about two hundred pounds. Scientists calculated that it was about six feet eight inches long and about thirty inches high—tiny for a *Tyrannosaurus rex,* which could grow to more than forty feet in length and fifteen feet high.

Could this have been a dinosaur family—mother, father, older brother, and baby sister? It is interesting to imagine the four of them stopping by the side of a shady stream to feast on a recent kill. Perhaps they were finishing up their meal when a group of larger tyrannosaurs came along, killed them, and claimed the territory as their own.

Allosaurus (AL-oh-soar-us), a twenty-foot-long meat eater that flourished in the Jurassic Period, a few million years before *Tyrannosaurus rex,* may have had a family life, too. Robert Bakker has discovered a few intriguing clues. These clues have led him to believe that he may have discovered an *Allosaurus* nesting site.

Here a large female tyrannosaur, her mate, and their two youngsters rest on a stream bank. Remains of a recent meal—a type of duckbill called *Edmontosaurus* (ed-MON-toh-soar-us)—lie nearby. Did the ferocious *Tyrannosaurus rex* form family groups? No one knows for sure.

In Wyoming, near Como Bluff, Dr. Bakker found a group of large bones that had been grooved by *Allosaurus* teeth. Surrounding the gnawed bones, he found broken teeth from *Allosaurus* of all ages—from adults right down to tiny infants. Dr. Bakker believes that at this site, more than 150 million years ago, *Allosaurus* adults carried a huge carcass home to their nest, and the whole family dined on it together.

But these stories of *Tyrannosaurus* and *Allosaurus* families are based on just a few small clues. For now, there is not enough evidence to give us a clear picture. The stories of our *Tyrannosaurus rex* and *Allosaurus* families may be as mistaken as Henry Fairfield Osborn's first story of *Oviraptor* as the egg thief.

Since the early 1800s, thousands of fossils of adult dinosaurs have been found, but even with all the latest discoveries, fossils of dinosaur eggs and babies are still rare. Nests and the embryos that make accurate identification possible are still extremely rare.

For *Oviraptor, Maiasaura,* and a handful of other dinosaurs, fossil nests, eggs, embryos, and babies have told us more about what their lives may have been like than anyone could have ever foretold. As for the tyrannosaurs, stegosaurs, and the hundreds of other types of dinosaurs, the clues that will shed light on *their* secret lives are still out there in the rocks, waiting to be found. Who knows what surprises the future may hold. One thing we can be sure of: As long as paleontologists continue to explore, they will continue to be alert for any evidence that will give us a more accurate and fuller understanding of the mysterious lives of dinosaurs.

SUGGESTED READING

BOOKS

Andrews, Roy Chapman. *The New Conquest of Central Asia*. New York: American Museum of Natural History, 1932.

Bishop, Nic. *Digging for Bird Dinosaurs: An Expedition to Madagascar*. Boston: Houghton Mifflin, 2000.

Horner, John. *Digging Dinosaurs*. New York: Workman Publishing, 1988.

———. *Dinosaur Lives*. New York: HarperCollins, 1997.

Norell, Mark A., Eugene S. Gaffney, and Lowell Dingus. *Discovering Dinosaurs in the American Museum of Natural History*. New York: Alfred A. Knopf, 1995.

Novacek, Michael. *Dinosaurs of the Flaming Cliffs*. New York: Doubleday, 1996.

Psihoyos, Louie. *Hunting Dinosaurs*. New York: Random House, 1994.

MAGAZINES

Chiappe, Luis M. "Dinosaur Embryos: Unscrambling the Past in Patagonia." *National Geographic* (December 1998).

———. "A Diversity of Early Birds." *Natural History* (June 1995).

Clark, James M. "An Egg Thief Exonerated." *Natural History* (June 1995).

Currie, Philip J. "The Great Dinosaur Egg Hunt." *National Geographic* (May 1996).

Norell, Mark A. "Origins of the Feathered Nest." *Natural History* (June 1995).

GLOSSARY

altricial: Describes an animal (usually a bird) that is born relatively helpless and needs a great deal of parental care in its early stages of development.

badlands: A dry landscape characterized by sparse plant life and intensely eroded hills.

bentonite: A type of clay made up of very fine particles that come from volcanic ash.

biped: An animal that walks or runs upright on two legs. Birds and human beings are bipeds.

brood: To sit on eggs in order to hatch them by means of body heat.

carnivorous: Describes any animal whose diet consists mainly of meat.

cartilage: The flexible milky-colored gristle that protects and cushions the ends of bones where, in adult animals, one bone forms a joint with another. In embryos, the skeleton is made up almost entirely of cartilage. As an embryo develops, most of the cartilage gradually turns into bone.

ceratopsian: Any of a group of large herbivorous, quadrupedal dinosaurs, distinguished by facial horns and frills. *Protoceratops* and *Triceratops* are ceratopsians.

clone: To make an exact copy of an animal using a single cell from that animal.

cold-blooded: Describes any animal whose body temperature varies with the temperature of its environment. Reptiles and amphibians are cold-blooded.

Cretaceous Period: The final third of the Mesozoic Era (the time of dinosaurs), about 144 to 65 million years ago. All dinosaurs died out by the end of the Cretaceous.

embryo: An animal in the very first stages of its development, before birth or hatching.

excavate: To carefully dig out and remove.

hadrosaur: A family of herbivorous, bipedal ornithopods with broad toothless beaks and multiple rows of grinding teeth.

herbivorous: Describes any animal that eats only plants.

hypsilophodont: A family of small to medium-size, herbivorous, bipedal ornithopods with horny beaks and upper front teeth that could bite against their beaks.

Jurassic Period: The middle third of the Mesozoic Era, from 206 to 144 million years ago.

lambeosaur: Any of a subgroup of hadrosaurs with complicated tubes or crests on the tops of their skulls.

ornithopod: Any of a diverse group of herbivorous, bipedal dinosaurs. Hadrosaurs and hypsilophodonts are ornithopods.

paleontologist: A scientist who studies the fossil remains of living organisms from past geological ages.

precocial: Describes an animal (usually a bird) that is born relatively strong and is independent right from birth.

preparator: A person who cleans and prepares specimens (usually fossils) for museum display.

quadruped: A type of animal that walks or runs primarily on four legs. Cows and crocodiles are quadrupeds.

rookery: A large colony where social birds or mammals gather to nest and raise their babies.

sauropod: Any of a group of huge, herbivorous, quadrupedal dinosaurs with long necks and tails and relatively small heads. All members of the titanosaur family are sauropods.

theropod: Any of a group of carnivorous, bipedal dinosaurs with bladelike teeth, clawed hands, three-toed clawed feet, and hollow limb bones. *Tyrannosaurus*, *Troodon*, and *Oviraptor* are theropods.

titanosaur: A family of Cretaceous sauropods with pencil-like teeth. Titanosaurs were the last-surviving members of the sauropod group.

Triassic Period: The first third of the Mesozoic Era, from 250 to 206 million years ago. Dinosaurs originated in the Triassic.

tyrannosaur: A family of theropods with large heads, small forearms with two-clawed hands, and long legs with three-toed feet.

warm-blooded: Describes any animal whose body temperature stays the same, regardless of the temperature of its environment. Birds and mammals are warm-blooded.

DINOSAUR DICTIONARY

Below are listed all the dinosaur genera mentioned in this book. A genus (plural: genera) is a group of species with a shared ancestry. Genus names are always italicized.

Albertosaurus: A theropod that lived during the Late Cretaceous. Member of the tyrannosaur family. Fossils found in western North America.

Allosaurus: A theropod that lived during the Late Jurassic. Fossils found in North America and East Africa.

Apatosaurus: A sauropod from the Late Jurassic. (Formerly known as *Brontosaurus*.) Fossils found in North America.

Archaeopteryx: An ancient bird from the Late Jurassic. Fossils found in Europe.

Argentinosaurus: An extremely large sauropod from the Late Cretaceous. Member of the titanosaur family. Fossils found in South America.

Deinonychus: A theropod from the Early Cretaceous. Fossils found in North America.

Drinker: A small ornithopod from the Late Jurassic. Member of the hypsilophodont family. Fossils found in North America.

Edmontosaurus: An ornithopod from the Late Cretaceous. Member of the hadrosaur family. Fossils found in North America.

Hylaeosaurus: A sauropod from the Late Cretaceous. Fossils found in Europe.

Hypacrosaurus: An ornithopod from the Late Cretaceous. Member of the lambeosaur family. Fossils found in North America.

Iguanodon: An ornithopod from the Early Cretaceous. Fossils found in Europe and North America.

Maiasaura: An ornithopod from the Late Cretaceous. Member of the hadrosaur family. Fossils found in North America.

Megalosaurus: A theropod from the Early Jurassic. Fossils found in Europe.

Neuquenosaurus: A sauropod from the Late Cretaceous. Member of the titanosaur family. Fossils found in South America.

Orodromeus: A small ornithopod from the Late Cretaceous. Member of the hypsilophodont family. Fossils found in North America.

Oviraptor: A small theropod from the Late Cretaceous. Fossils found in Asia.

Protoceratops: A small ceratopsian from the Late Cretaceous. Fossils found in Asia.

Saltasaurus: A medium-size sauropod from the Cretaceous. Member of the titanosaur family. Fossils found in South America.

Scipionyx: A theropod from the Cretaceous. Fossils found in Europe.

Stegosaurus: A thyreophoran from the Late Jurassic. Member of the stegosaur family. Fossils found in North America.

Troodon: A small theropod from the Late Cretaceous. Fossils found in North America.

Tyrannosaurus: A large theropod from the Late Cretaceous. Member of the tyrannosaur family. Fossils found in North America and Asia.

Velociraptor: A small theropod from the Late Cretaceous. Fossils found in Asia.

INDEX

Page numbers in **boldface** type refer to illustrations.